Growing up Safe

Safety
streetproofing

Illustrated by Sue Wilkinson

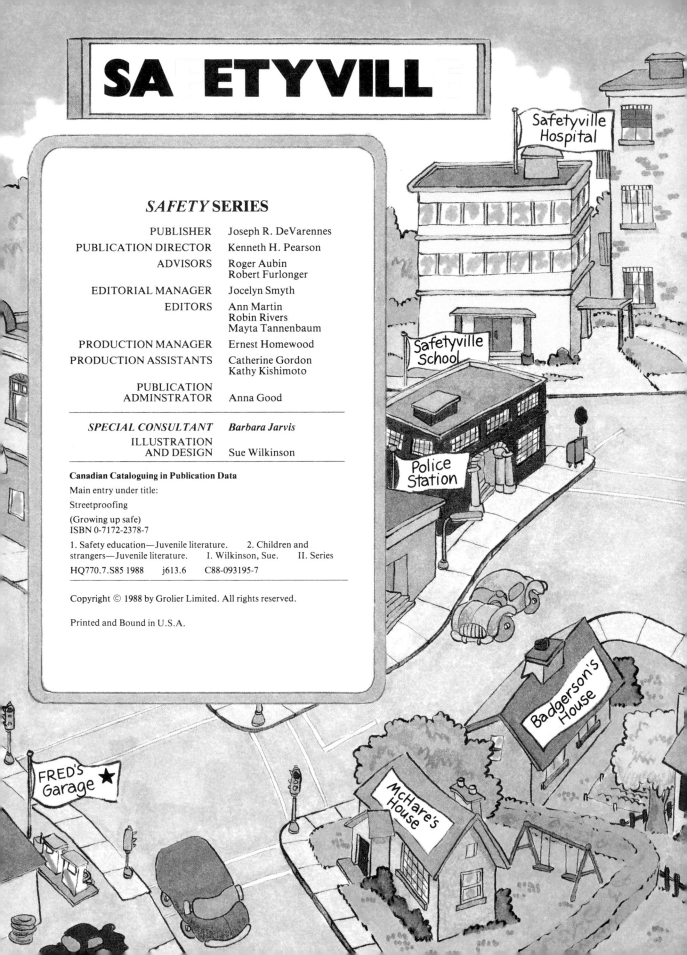

SA ETYVILL

SAFETY SERIES

PUBLISHER	Joseph R. DeVarennes
PUBLICATION DIRECTOR	Kenneth H. Pearson
ADVISORS	Roger Aubin
	Robert Furlonger
EDITORIAL MANAGER	Jocelyn Smyth
EDITORS	Ann Martin
	Robin Rivers
	Mayta Tannenbaum
PRODUCTION MANAGER	Ernest Homewood
PRODUCTION ASSISTANTS	Catherine Gordon
	Kathy Kishimoto
PUBLICATION ADMINSTRATOR	Anna Good

SPECIAL CONSULTANT	Barbara Jarvis
ILLUSTRATION AND DESIGN	Sue Wilkinson

Canadian Cataloguing in Publication Data

Main entry under title:

Streetproofing

(Growing up safe)
ISBN 0-7172-2378-7

1. Safety education—Juvenile literature.   2. Children and strangers—Juvenile literature.   I. Wilkinson, Sue.   II. Series

HQ770.7.S85 1988   j613.6   C88-093195-7

Come join Gina and Danny Raccoonelli as they find out everything they need to know about streetproofing safety.

IF A STRANGER ASKS YOU TO GO SOMEWHERE SAY NO.

ONLY OPEN THE DOOR BY YOURSELF TO SOMEONE YOU KNOW WELL.

GO TO THE PARK OR PLAYGROUND WITH YOUR PARENTS OR THE PERSON WHO IS LOOKING AFTER YOU.

NEVER GO FOR A RIDE WITH A STRANGER.

CHECK WITH YOUR PARENTS BEFORE TAKING A GIFT FROM ANYONE YOU DON'T KNOW WELL.

TELL YOUR TEACHER IF A STRANGER IS WAITING FOR YOU OUTSIDE SCHOOL.

IF YOU WANT TO GO OUT, ASK YOUR PARENTS OR THE PERSON WHO IS LOOKING AFTER YOU.

TELL YOUR PARENTS IF A STRANGER INVITES YOU ANYWHERE.

WHEN YOU ARE CONFUSED, ASK YOUR PARENTS FOR HELP.

THERE ARE MANY PEOPLE WHO TOUCH YOU, BUT IT SHOULD NEVER MAKE YOU FEEL UNCOMFORTABLE.

Mom, do I have to sit on Uncle Ricky's knee?

Not if it upsets you. I'll speak to him next time he visits.

Tell your mother or father if you don't like the way someone touches you.

NEVER PLAY IN DESERTED BUILDINGS.

LEARN THE NUMBER TO CALL IN CASE OF AN EMERGENCY.

It's important to learn your telephone number and address so people who can help when you're in trouble will know where to find you.

A BLOCK PARENT HOUSE IS A SAFE PLACE TO GO WHEN YOU ARE IN TROUBLE.

POLICE OFFICERS ARE YOUR FRIENDS AND HELP YOU TO STAY SAFE.